MW01487126

10 COLUMN Disbursement Journal

DISBURSEMENT JOURNAL

1	2	3	4	5	6	7	8	9	10

DISBURSEMENT JOURNAL

1	2	3	4	5	6	7	8	9	10

DISBURSEMENT JOURNAL

1	2	3	4	5	6	7	8	9	10

DISBURSEMENT JOURNAL

1	2	3	4	5	6	7	8	9	10

DISBURSEMENT JOURNAL

1	2	3	4	5	6	7	8	9	10

DISBURSEMENT JOURNAL

1	2	3	4	5	6	7	8	9	10

DISBURSEMENT JOURNAL

1	2	3	4	5	6	7	8	9	10

DISBURSEMENT JOURNAL

1	2	3	4	5	6	7	8	9	10

DISBURSEMENT JOURNAL

1	2	3	4	5	6	7	8	9	10

DISBURSEMENT JOURNAL

1	2	3	4	5	6	7	8	9	10

DISBURSEMENT JOURNAL

1	2	3	4	5	6	7	8	9	10

DISBURSEMENT JOURNAL

1	2	3	4	5	6	7	8	9	10

DISBURSEMENT JOURNAL

1	2	3	4	5	6	7	8	9	10

DISBURSEMENT JOURNAL

1	2	3	4	5	6	7	8	9	10

DISBURSEMENT JOURNAL

1	2	3	4	5	6	7	8	9	10

DISBURSEMENT JOURNAL

1	2	3	4	5	6	7	8	9	10

DISBURSEMENT JOURNAL

1	2	3	4	5	6	7	8	9	10

DISBURSEMENT JOURNAL

1	2	3	4	5	6	7	8	9	10

DISBURSEMENT JOURNAL

1	2	3	4	5	6	7	8	9	10

DISBURSEMENT JOURNAL

1	2	3	4	5	6	7	8	9	10

DISBURSEMENT JOURNAL

1	2	3	4	5	6	7	8	9	10

DISBURSEMENT JOURNAL

1	2	3	4	5	6	7	8	9	10

DISBURSEMENT JOURNAL

1	2	3	4	5	6	7	8	9	10

DISBURSEMENT JOURNAL

1	2	3	4	5	6	7	8	9	10

DISBURSEMENT JOURNAL

1	2	3	4	5	6	7	8	9	10

DISBURSEMENT JOURNAL

1	2	3	4	5	6	7	8	9	10

DISBURSEMENT JOURNAL

1	2	3	4	5	6	7	8	9	10

DISBURSEMENT JOURNAL

1	2	3	4	5	6	7	8	9	10

DISBURSEMENT JOURNAL

1	2	3	4	5	6	7	8	9	10

DISBURSEMENT JOURNAL

1	2	3	4	5	6	7	8	9	10

DISBURSEMENT JOURNAL

1	2	3	4	5	6	7	8	9	10

DISBURSEMENT JOURNAL

1	2	3	4	5	6	7	8	9	10

DISBURSEMENT JOURNAL

1	2	3	4	5	6	7	8	9	10

DISBURSEMENT JOURNAL

1	2	3	4	5	6	7	8	9	10

DISBURSEMENT JOURNAL

1	2	3	4	5	6	7	8	9	10

DISBURSEMENT JOURNAL

1	2	3	4	5	6	7	8	9	10

DISBURSEMENT JOURNAL

1	2	3	4	5	6	7	8	9	10

DISBURSEMENT JOURNAL

1	2	3	4	5	6	7	8	9	10

DISBURSEMENT JOURNAL

1	2	3	4	5	6	7	8	9	10

DISBURSEMENT JOURNAL

1	2	3	4	5	6	7	8	9	10

DISBURSEMENT JOURNAL

1	2	3	4	5	6	7	8	9	10

DISBURSEMENT JOURNAL

1	2	3	4	5	6	7	8	9	10

DISBURSEMENT JOURNAL

1	2	3	4	5	6	7	8	9	10

DISBURSEMENT JOURNAL

1	2	3	4	5	6	7	8	9	10

DISBURSEMENT JOURNAL

1	2	3	4	5	6	7	8	9	10

DISBURSEMENT JOURNAL

1	2	3	4	5	6	7	8	9	10

DISBURSEMENT JOURNAL

1	2	3	4	5	6	7	8	9	10

DISBURSEMENT JOURNAL

1	2	3	4	5	6	7	8	9	10

DISBURSEMENT JOURNAL

1	2	3	4	5	6	7	8	9	10

DISBURSEMENT JOURNAL

1	2	3	4	5	6	7	8	9	10

DISBURSEMENT JOURNAL

1	2	3	4	5	6	7	8	9	10

DISBURSEMENT JOURNAL

1	2	3	4	5	6	7	8	9	10

DISBURSEMENT JOURNAL

1	2	3	4	5	6	7	8	9	10

DISBURSEMENT JOURNAL

1	2	3	4	5	6	7	8	9	10

DISBURSEMENT JOURNAL

1	2	3	4	5	6	7	8	9	10

DISBURSEMENT JOURNAL

1	2	3	4	5	6	7	8	9	10

DISBURSEMENT JOURNAL

1	2	3	4	5	6	7	8	9	10

DISBURSEMENT JOURNAL

1	2	3	4	5	6	7	8	9	10

DISBURSEMENT JOURNAL

1	2	3	4	5	6	7	8	9	10

DISBURSEMENT JOURNAL

1	2	3	4	5	6	7	8	9	10

DISBURSEMENT JOURNAL

1	2	3	4	5	6	7	8	9	10

DISBURSEMENT JOURNAL

1	2	3	4	5	6	7	8	9	10

DISBURSEMENT JOURNAL

1	2	3	4	5	6	7	8	9	10

DISBURSEMENT JOURNAL

1	2	3	4	5	6	7	8	9	10

DISBURSEMENT JOURNAL

1	2	3	4	5	6	7	8	9	10

DISBURSEMENT JOURNAL

1	2	3	4	5	6	7	8	9	10

DISBURSEMENT JOURNAL

1	2	3	4	5	6	7	8	9	10

DISBURSEMENT JOURNAL

1	2	3	4	5	6	7	8	9	10

DISBURSEMENT JOURNAL

1	2	3	4	5	6	7	8	9	10

DISBURSEMENT JOURNAL

1	2	3	4	5	6	7	8	9	10

DISBURSEMENT JOURNAL

1	2	3	4	5	6	7	8	9	10

DISBURSEMENT JOURNAL

1	2	3	4	5	6	7	8	9	10

DISBURSEMENT JOURNAL

1	2	3	4	5	6	7	8	9	10

DISBURSEMENT JOURNAL

1	2	3	4	5	6	7	8	9	10

DISBURSEMENT JOURNAL

1	2	3	4	5	6	7	8	9	10

DISBURSEMENT JOURNAL

1	2	3	4	5	6	7	8	9	10

DISBURSEMENT JOURNAL

1	2	3	4	5	6	7	8	9	10

DISBURSEMENT JOURNAL

1	2	3	4	5	6	7	8	9	10

DISBURSEMENT JOURNAL

1	2	3	4	5	6	7	8	9	10

DISBURSEMENT JOURNAL

1	2	3	4	5	6	7	8	9	10

DISBURSEMENT JOURNAL

1	2	3	4	5	6	7	8	9	10

DISBURSEMENT JOURNAL

1	2	3	4	5	6	7	8	9	10

DISBURSEMENT JOURNAL

1	2	3	4	5	6	7	8	9	10

DISBURSEMENT JOURNAL

1	2	3	4	5	6	7	8	9	10

DISBURSEMENT JOURNAL

1	2	3	4	5	6	7	8	9	10

DISBURSEMENT JOURNAL

1	2	3	4	5	6	7	8	9	10

DISBURSEMENT JOURNAL

1	2	3	4	5	6	7	8	9	10

DISBURSEMENT JOURNAL

1	2	3	4	5	6	7	8	9	10

DISBURSEMENT JOURNAL

1	2	3	4	5	6	7	8	9	10

DISBURSEMENT JOURNAL

1	2	3	4	5	6	7	8	9	10

DISBURSEMENT JOURNAL

1	2	3	4	5	6	7	8	9	10

DISBURSEMENT JOURNAL

1	2	3	4	5	6	7	8	9	10

DISBURSEMENT JOURNAL

1	2	3	4	5	6	7	8	9	10

DISBURSEMENT JOURNAL

1	2	3	4	5	6	7	8	9	10

DISBURSEMENT JOURNAL

1	2	3	4	5	6	7	8	9	10

DISBURSEMENT JOURNAL

1	2	3	4	5	6	7	8	9	10

DISBURSEMENT JOURNAL

1		2		3		4		5		6		7		8		9		10		

DISBURSEMENT JOURNAL

1	2	3	4	5	6	7	8	9	10

Made in United States
North Haven, CT
07 July 2024

54481022R00057